*Cornerstones of Freedom*

*The Story of*

# The Iran Hostage Crisis

R. Conrad Stein

CHILDRENS PRESS®
CHICAGO

**Library of Congress Cataloging-in-Publication Data**

Stein, R. Conrad.
    The Iran hostage crisis / by R. Conrad Stein.
      p.  cm. — (Cornerstones of freedom)
Includes bibliographical references.
   ISBN 0-516-06681-1
   1. Iran Hostage Crisis, 1979–1981—Juvenile literature. I.
Title.  II. Series.
E183.8.I55S73  1994
955.05′4—dc20                 94-9492
                          CIP
                          AC

Tehran, Iran. November 4, 1979.

From his office window at the American embassy, the diplomat Moorhead Kennedy, Jr., looked out at a sea of angry faces. A mob of at least five hundred Iranian demonstrators stood on the street, chanting as if they were at a football game. But instead of cheers, they shouted out curses: "Death to Carter!" "Death to America!" "Death to the Shah!" As he watched the Iranians burning the American flag, Kennedy realized that he and the many other Americans in the embassy were in serious danger. He later said, "I looked down on all the noise and anti-American anger, and I wondered to myself what it would be like to die."

Moorhead Kennedy, Jr.

An angry Iranian mob burns the American flag in a demonstration in Tehran, Iran.

*President Jimmy Carter*

Hostile crowds had gathered every day for two weeks since President Jimmy Carter allowed the former Shah of Iran to enter the United States. The Shah (another word for king) was the hated ex-dictator of Iran. Carter had let him come to America because he was suffering from cancer and needed medical treatment. In the opinion of the Iranian demonstrators, Carter had aided the devil himself.

One of the protesters began climbing the iron bars of the embassy gate. Others followed. Most of the demonstrators were young, athletic college students. In minutes, fifty or more swarmed over the gate and were rushing the embassy building.

A detail of thirteen U.S. Marines guarded the embassy. They had received orders not to fire their weapons, regardless of what the protesters did. Retreating into the embassy, the marines threw tear gas grenades, but the rampaging Iranians broke windows and infiltrated the compound. Marine Sergeant James Lopez said, "To put it bluntly all hell broke loose, and we couldn't stop it."

*The scene in Tehran just after militant Iranian students had infiltrated the embassy*

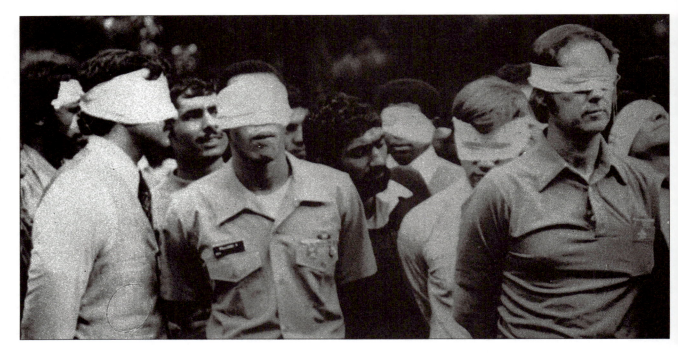

*November 4, 1979: Americans are paraded before the world's cameras by their Iranian captors.*

Iranian television crews arrived and filmed the students rounding up the American embassy workers. The embassy was a complex of several buildings, so the Iranians herded all the Americans to central locations. The Americans' hands were tied behind their backs, and they were blindfolded. These terrifying images soon reached the rest of the world on satellite television.

In Washington, D.C., President Jimmy Carter received an urgent telephone call informing him that fifty to sixty Americans had been seized. Carter later wrote, "[At first] we were deeply disturbed, but reasonably confident that the Iranian authorities would soon remove the attackers from the embassy compound and release our people."

To Carter's dismay, a quick settlement did not come. The Iranian government was terribly disorganized, and the students were allowed to carry on with their outrageous actions. One tense day followed another, and hatred toward America mushroomed throughout Iran. The students had won wild support from the Iranian people. As Carter said, "They [the students] had become overnight heroes in Iran."

Iran shared a northern border with the Soviet Union, and it was a nation rich with oil. For these reasons, the United States had long attempted to influence Iran's government. In 1941, the U.S. and its British allies helped install the then twenty-two-year-old Shah of Iran to power because Iranian oil was needed to defeat Nazi Germany. After World War II, the Shah

*President Carter (back facing camera) holds an emergency meeting in the Oval Office of the White House.*

*Tehran, Iran*

*The Iranian economy relied on its oil industry.*

remained at the head of government, but most Iranians considered him to be a puppet with Americans controlling his strings. The Shah used Iran's oil wealth to amass a personal fortune large enough to make him one of the richest men in the world. Also, with American blessings, he bought the latest and best planes and tanks for his armed forces. Meanwhile, millions of Iranians lived in miserable poverty.

*The Shah of Iran*

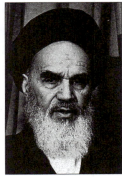

*Under the rule of the Shah, millions of Iranians suffered in poverty for years. Religious leader Ayatollah Khomeini (below) led a revolt to overthrow the Shah and his government.*

A religious upheaval swept the nation in the early 1970s. Iran is an Islamic land, where 98 percent of the people follow the Islamic faith. A stern Muslim leader named Ayatollah Ruholla Khomeini called for the overthrow of the Shah, the end of American influence, and the restoration of a religious state in Iran. The Shah attempted to crush the Ayatollah's religious revolt with his powerful army and a brutal secret police force called the SAVAK. But the violent anti-government demonstrations continued to threaten his government.

On January 16, 1979, with labor strikes and urban riots rocking the country, the Shah fled

*Demonstrators in Tehran toppled a statue of the Shah's father moments after the Shah fled Iran on January 16, 1979.*

to Egypt. He would never again return to Iran. The Iranian government fell into the hands of religious leaders headed by the Ayatollah Khomeini. Crowds in the streets celebrated the Shah's downfall, and anger toward America became a national passion. President Carter's decision to allow the Shah into the United States triggered the embassy takeover. A long and horrible nightmare followed.

Terror reigned inside the embassy after its seizure on November 4. American captives were

*When Jimmy Carter allowed the Shah to enter the United States, angry and violent demonstrations broke out both in Iran (above) and in Washington, D.C. (left).*

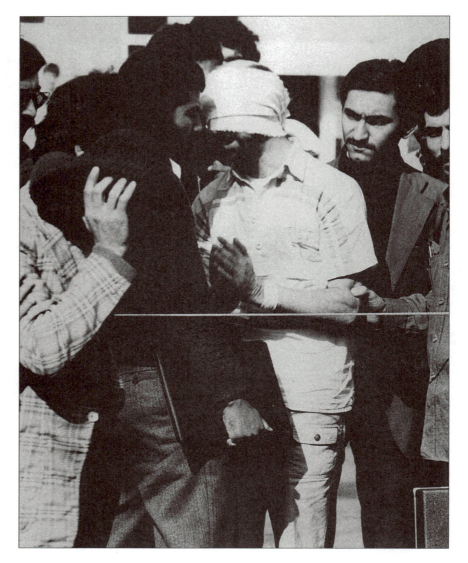

beaten and threatened at gunpoint. Elizabeth Montagne, a forty-one-year-old secretary, was confronted by a gunman who demanded that she open the embassy's safe. She told him, truthfully, she did not know the combination. The gunman loaded a revolver with one bullet and pressed the pistol against her heart.

Montagne later recalled, "He went click, and

the bullet went up one chamber."

"Is this worth dying for?" he asked.

"I said, 'No, it's not,' and he went click, and the bullet went up another notch."

This cruel game of Russian roulette went on for five minutes. To Elizabeth Montagne, it seemed an eternity. "The only thing I could think of was, 'I wonder what it would feel like to have a bullet go through my chest.'"

In Washington, President Carter and his staff tried to untangle the confused reports filtering into his office. No one was certain who controlled the fate of the American captives— the militant students or the Iranian government. Nobody knew what the kidnappers hoped to gain by taking hostages. Several Iranian spokesmen demanded the return of the Shah so they could try him in court as a criminal. Carter refused to send the Shah back against his will. Such an act would mean the United States had paid ransom to international kidnappers. It would set a precedent, and all terrorists would feel they could blackmail the American government by committing similar crimes.

President Carter and his staff were most disturbed by the veiled threats coming from Iran that the revolutionary government was considering trying all the American hostages as spies. Under Islamic law, convicted spies are put to death.

On the banner: CARTER IS SUPPORTING THIS NAS[T]... CRIMINAL UNDER THE PRETEXT OF SI[...]

OPPRESSED BLACKS !! THE UNITED STATS GOVERN[M]ENT IS OUR COMMON ENEMY

WE CONSIDER AMERICAN PEOP[LE] [AND] THE U.S. GOV[ERNME]NT [AS] TWO DIFFERE[NT] [...] Imam Khomeini

*The thirteen freed Americans speak to the press moments after being released from captivity.*

On November 19 and 20, the Iranian militants released thirteen hostages—five women and eight black men. One militant said the women were freed because "Islamic warriors do not wage war against women." The blacks were released because they were "an oppressed minority." Curiously, the Iranians kept one black man and two women. These three, a spokesman said, were deemed to be spies.

The remaining hostages—now a total of fifty-three—were split into random groups and held in different places on the embassy grounds. Some were jammed into pitch-dark closets where they remained for days. Those held in groups were

14

forbidden to talk or even to make eye contact with each other. The largest band was imprisoned in the basement of the main embassy building. The hostages' hands were tied day and night.

"It was like living in a tomb," said one hostage. "You didn't hear the outside world. You didn't see the outside world. You didn't know what was going on at all. You were completely cut off."

The United Nations and the World Court issued harsh statements denouncing the embassy takeover. Egyptian President Anwar Sadat, himself a Muslim, said, "There is no basis in Islam for this. Islam does not justify the taking of hostages."

A dreary Christmas marked the 52nd day of captivity for the hostages. Three million

*United Nations Secretary General Kurt Waldheim (left) denounced the Iranians' actions, but asked the U.S. to avoid any action that would inflame the crisis.*

*Reverend William Howard (right) was one of three clergymen to visit the hostages on Christmas.*

Americans sent cards to the captives, but the guards allowed only a few to reach their prisoners. The militants did permit three American clergymen to enter the embassy grounds. The hostages and ministers sang carols and prayed together. One of the clergyman said, "There were tears in their eyes. There were tears in our eyes. I pray to God they will be released as soon as possible."

From the beginning of the hostage crisis, President Carter publicly ruled out a military rescue attempt. Tehran lay more than 250 miles inland and was surrounded by deserts and mountains. It would be impossible, the president claimed, for a rescue mission to penetrate that far into a hostile country and bring the captives to safety.

But in secret, a special commando team based at Fort Bragg, North Carolina, had been practicing a rescue operation since the first week of the hostage crisis. In April 1980, President Carter gave final approval to a daring plan designed to liberate the hostages.

Under the cover of darkness on April 24, 1980, eight Sea Stallion helicopters lifted off from the aircraft carrier *Nimitz* in the Arabian Sea. The helicopters flew toward an abandoned airstrip in the Iranian desert that the American commanders had called Desert One. The helicopters were to rendezvous at Desert One with six giant C-130 Hercules transport planes that had taken off from Egypt. The complex operation involved two hundred army, navy, marine, and air force commandos. After linking up at Desert One, their mission was to go to Tehran, infiltrate the embassy prison, free the hostages, and fly them home.

*A Sea Stallion helicopter takes off from a U.S. aircraft carrier.*

Less than an hour after it left the *Nimitz,* one of the Sea Stallion helicopters developed rotor blade problems and had to land in the desert. Its crew was picked up by another helicopter. The mission continued, but the helicopter pilots struggled through a blinding sandstorm. Another Sea Stallion suffered damage to its navigation equipment and was forced to return to the carrier. Six of the original eight helicopters landed at Desert One more than an hour behind schedule.

The worst was yet to come.

The airstrip lay in a remote region linked to the nearest city by a little-used desert road. It was thought no one would see the assembled helicopters and transport planes. Yet that night a fuel truck, a van, and a bus full of Iranian passengers rumbled down the road directly into the midst of American operations. The commandos fired warning shots, and the fuel truck burst into flames. The driver scrambled out, entered the van, and raced away into the night. The commandos cursed their luck, thinking the driver would tell Iranian authorities about the invasion. The bus and all its passengers were captured by the Americans.

The mission continued to disintegrate. Mission commander Colonel Charles Beckwith learned a third helicopter was also disabled. This left him with only five Sea Stallions.

*Colonel*
*Charles Beckwith*

18

"My God, I'm going to fail," Beckwith said to himself. With a grim sense of dejection, Colonel Beckwith decided to cancel the mission and fly back to the carrier.

As one of the helicopters lifted off the desert floor, its blades stirred up a tremendous whirlpool of dust. The pilot of the chopper drifted toward a Hercules transport plane parked on the ground. He probably could not see the aircraft. "We had all this dust coming down from the rotors," said Sergeant Joseph Beyers, who was inside the transport plane. "There was just too much dust and stuff flying around." The rotor blades of the Sea Stallion slashed into the parked transport plane, and both aircraft exploded into flames. Sergeant Beyers was pulled from the wreckage, badly

*Sergeant Joseph Beyers*

*The rescue mission ended in disaster as eight Americans lost their lives in a fiery desert collision.*

*Hamilton Jordan*

burned but alive. His comrades were not so lucky. Eight Americans died in the collision. The survivors were flown to safety, leaving behind the twisted hulks of aircraft and the charred remains of American bodies.

Hamilton Jordan, the president's closest aide, was with Jimmy Carter when he received a phone call telling him the mission had failed and American lives were lost. "The President closed his eyes," Jordan reported. "His jaw dropped and his face turned ashen. . . . No one said a word. The harsh reality of the failed mission and the tragic deaths began to sink in. Finally Cyrus Vance [the secretary of state] broke the stillness, 'Mr. President, I'm very, very sorry.'"

After the rescue attempt, the hostages were dispersed to houses in the Iranian countryside. With the hostages spread out, another rescue mission would be impossible.

On the 250th day of the kidnapping ordeal, Iran released one hostage. Richard Queen, a twenty-eight-year-old consular officer, had contracted the grave disease multiple sclerosis. Iran announced it was setting Queen free as a "humanitarian gesture." Queen's release reduced the number of American hostages to fifty-two.

*Abolhassan Bani-Sadr*

On July 27, 1980, the 267th day, the Shah of Iran died in a hospital in Egypt. Logic dictated that the captives should now be set free, but Iran made no such gesture. Instead, Iranian radio simply announced, "The bloodsucker of the century has died at last."

In late September 1980, Iran and neighbor Iraq went to war over a border dispute. Iran's president, Abolhassan Bani-Sadr, claimed the U.S. was behind the war and warned, "If [the war] gets worse, it will also get worse for the hostages."

*Among the dignitaries at the Shah's funeral in Cairo, Egypt, was Richard Nixon (far right), ex-president of the United States.*

The American kidnap victims were unaware of the events going on outside their cells. They faced a day-to-day struggle to cope with imprisonment. Some survived by making a game of frustrating their guards. To befuddle the student militants, groups of hostages would suddenly bark like dogs or meow like cats. Two marines who were farmers in civilian life practiced hog calls to each other, much to the exasperation of the Iranians. Marine Sergeant Rodney Sickman regularly beat his guards in arm-wrestling contests. One night a powerfully built Iranian challenged him to a real wrestling match. Sickman threw the man across the room, sending him crashing into a brick wall. "They had to take him to a hospital, and he came back with a sling on his arm," Sickman said.

*Sergeant Rodney "Rocky" Sickman*

For the most part, the captives were forbidden to talk to one another, but they still found ingenious ways to communicate. "We would leave notes in the toilet paper rolls, under the toilet, in the sink, behind a mirror, or under a loose tile," said Marine Sergeant James Lopez. "And we had a telegraph system, knocking on walls." Lopez also amused his fellow captives by drawing pictures. The Iranian guards failed to recognize that the pictures were actually cartoons lampooning them. One showed an Iranian guard with bats flying near his head, implying the man was crazy, or "batty."

*Emotions in America ran from bitter anger to fervent hope throughout the hostage ordeal. While some Americans took to the streets to vent their anger at Iran (opposite page), others hung yellow ribbons (right) to express their hope for the hostages' quick release. In Hermitage, Pennsylvania (above), a new American flag was raised on every day the hostages were held.*

In the United States, feelings of sympathy toward the hostages and rage against Iran intensified. Iranian students were shunned on college campuses, and Iranian workers were fired from their jobs for no good reason. A popular song contained the lines: "Bomb, bomb, bomb . . . bomb, bomb Iran!" Yellow ribbons became a symbol of a nation keeping faith with the captives. Along streets throughout the country, yellow ribbons were tied to trees and light posts. At a field near the town of Hermitage, Pennsylvania, people raised a new American flag each day of the crisis. The flags were donated by concerned Americans from practically every state.

The hostage situation was an unstated but powerful campaign issue in the 1980 presidential contest between Jimmy Carter and Ronald Reagan. Because delicate negotiations were taking place with the Iranian government,

*President
Ronald Reagan*

neither candidate came out with a specific plan to free the captives. Still, American helplessness over the matter lingered in voters' minds. On November 4, 1980—precisely one year after student militants attacked the embassy—Americans went to the polls and elected Ronald Reagan president by a huge majority of votes. It is impossible to determine the full impact that the situation in Iran had in Carter's defeat, but most political experts agree that the hostage crisis cost Carter the presidency.

Another Christmas passed, and the fifty-two hostages remained in prison. But now negotiations with the Iranians began to produce results. The Iranians were primarily concerned with money. At the beginning of the crisis, President Carter had seized all Iranian money held in U.S. banks, most of which had come from oil sales. The Iranian government desperately needed those frozen funds to carry on its war with Iraq. Negotiators decided that the U.S. would release $7.9 billion to Iran, and a deal was struck to release the hostages.

In Iran, guards entered the various cells announcing, "Pack up. It's time. You're going home." Many hostages believed it was another Iranian trick to demoralize them. They were again tied up and blindfolded. As a final insult, guards pushed and punched the Americans as they were herded into buses. They were then driven to the airport, and they boarded an Algerian airplane. Next came a long and nerve-racking wait on the runway. The Americans still refused to let their hopes for freedom run wild. When the engines finally started and the plane rumbled down the runway, one of the hostages whispered, "It's true, we're really going home."

After 444 days and a tense airplane ride out of Iran, the hostages finally stepped onto friendly soil when they landed in West Germany.

The final release date fell on January 20, 1981, after the fifty-two Americans had spent 444 days as prisoners. That same day, Ronald Reagan was slated to take the oath of office and become president. In Washington, D.C., people lined the streets to watch the inaugural parade, but news reports around the country focused more on the hostages' release.

The hostages were flown from Iran to the American airbase at Wiesbaden, West Germany. After medical exams, they were greeted by Jimmy Carter.

*Jimmy Carter greets ex-hostage Bruce Laingen.*

The released hostages recovered from their ordeal at the U.S. military hospital in Wiesbaden, West Germany. Former president Carter (left photo, waving) officially welcomed the Americans back to freedom, and the ex-hostages (above) greeted Carter like a hero.

*Back in the U.S., Moorhead Kennedy (above, waving) and other ex-hostages are anxious to be reunited with family and friends. A jubilant parade through Washington, D.C., followed their return.*

*Rocky Sickman arrives safe at home in Missouri, much to the delight of his father.*

Despite the anxiety and political trouble the crisis had caused Jimmy Carter, he maintained that some good had emerged from the nightmare. He told the freed captives of the yellow ribbons and the millions of letters he received from ordinary Americans worried about their fate. He claimed the long and terrible ordeal had strengthened the nation as a family, a family where an injury to one is felt as an injury to all. The ex-president said, "This crisis has unified our nation and our people like nothing in my lifetime since World War II."

## INDEX

## PHOTO CREDITS

Cover, Illustration by Heidi Schmeck; 1, Courtesy Penelope Laingen; 2, 3 (bottom), AP/Wide World; 3 (top), 4, UPI/Bettmann; 5, AP/Wide World; 6, 7 (top), UPI/Bettmann; 7 (bottom), © Christine Osborne/ Valan Photos; 8 (bottom), Stock Montage, Inc.; 8 (top), 9 (top), SuperStock International; 9 (bottom), AP/Wide World; 10, 11, (both photos), UPI/Bettmann; 12, AP/Wide World; 14, UPI/Bettmann; 15, 16, AP/Wide World; 17, Courtesy Department of Defense; 18, 19 (top), UPI/Bettmann; 19 (bottom), 20, AP/Wide World; 21, 22 (both photos), 23, UPI/Bettmann; 24, Courtesy Avenue of 444 Flags Foundation, Hermitage, Pennsylvania; 24 (bottom), SuperStock International; 25, AP/Wide World; 26, SuperStock International; 27, UPI/Bettmann; 28, 29 (both photos), 30 (top), AP/Wide World; 30 (bottom), 31, UPI/Bettmann

Picture Identifications:
page 1: Penne Laingen (with sons Chip and Jim) ties a yellow ribbon around a tree in her front yard as she hopes for the safety of her husband, hostage Bruce Laingen.
page 2: The Ayatollah Khomeini is swarmed by an adoring crowd in Tehran, Iran.

Project Editors: Shari Joffe and Mark Friedman
Design and Electronic Composition: TJS Design
Photo Editor: Jan Izzo
Cornerstones of Freedom Logo: David Cunningham

## ABOUT THE AUTHOR

**R. Conrad Stein** was born and grew up in Chicago. He graduated from the University of Illinois with a degree in history, and he later studied in Mexico. He is the author of more than eighty published books for young readers.

Like millions of other Americans, Mr. Stein felt frustrated and angry during the 444 days of the Iranian hostage crisis. He remembers it as a dark period in American history.